INSURING THE FUTURE

A MILLENNIAL'S GUIDE TO UNDERSTANDING INSURANCE THROUGH THE LENS OF DIGITAL TOOLS AND SOCIAL MEDIA PLATFORMS

HITESH SAINI

Made with ♥ on the Notion Press Platform
www.notionpress.com

Dear Mr. Patrick Kelahan,I want to express my heartfelt gratitude to you for igniting my passion for insurance and showing me its immense value. Your guidance, wisdom, and mentorship have been invaluable in shaping my understanding of the field. This book would not have been possible without your guidance and support.

To Ms. Sandhya Suri, thank you for refining my words and helping me shape this book. Your keen eye for detail and commitment to excellence have been instrumental in ensuring the quality of this work.

To my teachers at Manipal Bangalore thank you for equipping me with knowledge and skills in the field of insurance. Your dedication and commitment to educating the next generation of insurance professionals are truly inspiring.

To my parents, Mr. Tirlok Chand Saini and Mrs. Kanta Saini I am forever grateful for providing me with an education that gave me the foundation to pursue my dreams. Without your support, encouragement, and guidance, I would not be where I am today.

To my wife Kavita, thank you for being my constant source of love, support, and inspiration. Your unwavering belief in me has been the driving force behind my pursuit of this book.

To my kids Pinank and Dhruvit, who gave me the strength to fight through the tough times when I battled cancer, thank you for being my lifeline. Your presence in my life has been a constant reminder of what truly matters.

To my younger brother Saurabh, and youngest brother Akshay, thank you for being a part of my life's journey. Your love, support, and encouragement have been instrumental in keeping me motivated and focused on my goals.

And to Kshitiz Sir, thank you for always pushing me to write and motivating me to follow my passion. Your belief in my abilities has been a constant source of inspiration.

To my dear friends and colleagues at the National Insurance Academy (NIA) –
Lakshaya, Kabeer, Nainy, Luv, and Renga – thank you for being my support
system throughout my time at the institution. Your encouragement, guidance,
and companionship made my journey of learning about insurance more
enjoyable and fulfilling.

And to the entire NIA family, thank you for the love and support you have given
me. Your contributions have been invaluable in shaping me into the person I am
today, and I will always cherish the memories and experiences I have gained
from being a part of this esteemed institution.

This book is dedicated to all of you, who have played a significant role in my life
and inspired me to write this book on insurance. I hope that this book will
inspire others to appreciate the value of insurance and make informed
decisions that will benefit them and their loved ones.

With deepest gratitude,

Hitesh Saini

Contents

Foreword

"I have had the privilege of being a mentor to the author of this book, and I am proud to say that I have seen him grow and develop into a skilled insurance professional. In this book, he shares his knowledge and expertise in the field of insurance with readers, providing them with insights into the importance of insurance and how it can benefit them.

Insurance is a complex and often misunderstood industry, but the author has done an excellent job of breaking down the jargon and explaining the various concepts in a simple and understandable way. His passion for the subject shines through in every chapter, and I have no doubt that this book will be a valuable resource for anyone looking to learn about insurance.

In addition to providing an overview of the various types of insurance available, the author has also included practical tips on how to choose the right coverage, file claims, and maximize savings through discounts and loyalty programs. This book is not just a theoretical guide but a practical tool that readers can use to make informed decisions about their insurance needs.

This book is particularly useful for teenagers who are starting to navigate the world of insurance. It breaks down the complex concepts in a way that is easy to understand, making it an excellent resource for anyone new to the industry. The author also includes real-life examples and practical tips that will help teenagers choose the right coverage for their needs.

This book is not just a theoretical guide but a practical tool that teenagers can use to make informed decisions about their insurance needs. It also emphasizes the importance of understanding the risks and benefits associated with different insurance policies, which is essential for anyone who wants to protect their financial future.

Overall, this book is a valuable resource that will help teenagers understand the importance of insurance and how it can benefit them. I highly recommend it to anyone who wants to learn more about this critical aspect of personal finance.

I would like to congratulate the author on this achievement and thank him for acknowledging the people who have played a significant role in his life. I hope this book inspires and educates readers and helps them make informed decisions about their insurance needs."

Patrick Kelahan

Insurance Consultant and Mentor

Preface

As I started my career in the insurance industry, I was fortunate enough to have mentors who taught me the value and importance of insurance. However, as I observed the younger generation, I noticed a lack of interest and understanding of insurance. This realization prompted me to write this book.

During my time at Manipal, I had the opportunity to learn about insurance in a structured and academic environment. It was there that I gained a strong foundation in the principles of insurance and the various types of coverage available.

Later, I had the privilege of working for HDFC, a leading insurance company in India. At HDFC, I had hands-on experience in the industry, learning the ins and outs of underwriting, policy administration, and claims management. This experience helped me understand the practical aspects of insurance and how it functions in the real world.

Eventually, I joined Policy Bazaar, India's largest insurance aggregator, where I honed my skills in digital marketing and customer engagement. This experience gave me insights into how consumers approach insurance and the challenges they face in understanding the nuances of coverage.

It was this combination of academic training and practical experience that inspired me to write this book. As I saw more and more millennials neglecting insurance, I realized that there was a need for a resource that explained insurance in their language and addressed their specific concerns.

Through this book, I aim to empower readers to make informed decisions about their insurance needs, whether it be for health, travel, home, or auto insurance. I hope that this book will serve as a valuable resource for anyone looking to learn about insurance and understand the benefits that it provides.

Thank you for choosing to read this book, and I hope that it proves to be informative and useful for you.

CHAPTER ONE

Insurance Basics Explained through Social Media Platforms

Insurance policies can be thought of as social media profiles, with each policy designed to protect a specific aspect of your life. Just as you have different profiles on Facebook, Instagram, Twitter, and LinkedIn, you have various insurance policies to cover your health, car, home, life, and more. These policies help you build a comprehensive financial safety net, just as social media profiles help you build a digital presence.

Premiums, deductibles, and coverage: The currency of the insurance world

Premiums, deductibles, and coverage amounts are essential components of insurance policies. In the context of social media, think of premiums as the "subscription fees" you pay to maintain your insurance policy. Deductibles can be compared to the "cost" of posting on social media, which might include the time and effort you put into creating content. The coverage amount is similar to the "reach" or "impact" of your posts, determining how much protection you have in case of a loss or event.

Comparing insurance types to social media platforms: Facebook, Instagram, Twitter, and more

Each insurance type can be compared to a different social media platform, based on the unique features and characteristics they offer.

Life Insurance (LinkedIn): Life insurance is like LinkedIn, as it focuses on securing your financial future and providing for your loved ones. Just as LinkedIn helps you build professional connections and advance your career, life insurance offers long-term financial protection for your family.

Health Insurance (Instagram): Health insurance can be compared to Instagram, where the focus is on wellness and maintaining a healthy lifestyle. Just as Instagram highlights curated snapshots of people's lives, health insurance offers a safety net for when you need medical care, ensuring you're financially protected against health-related expenses.

Auto Insurance (Twitter): Auto insurance is like Twitter, a platform known for its fast-paced nature and real-time updates. Similarly, auto insurance offers immediate financial protection in case of accidents or damages, ensuring you're not left stranded due to unforeseen events.

Home and Renters Insurance (Facebook): Home and renters insurance can be likened to Facebook, a platform that connects people to their communities and personal interests. Just as Facebook helps you share updates about your life and home, home and renters insurance provides financial protection for your living space and belongings.

Premiums are similar to the subscription fees you pay to access your favorite streaming platform or online game. These payments are made to the insurance company to obtain coverage, and they can be paid on a monthly, quarterly, or annual basis, depending on the policy. The cost of premiums is determined by various factors, such as the type of insurance, the coverage amount, and personal details like age and health. For example, a teenager who just started driving might pay a higher premium for car insurance compared to someone with more driving experience.

Deductibles, on the other hand, are like the initial payment you make when purchasing a new phone or gadget. When filing an insurance claim, you must pay the deductible amount before the insurance company steps in to cover the remaining expenses. For *instance, if you accidentally damage your phone and it costs $500 to repair, and your insurance has a $100 deductible, you would pay the $100, and the insurance company would cover the remaining $400. Choosing a higher deductible can result in lower premium costs, but it's essential to ensure you can afford the deductible if you need to file a claim.*

Coverage is similar to the protective case you put on your phone, safeguarding your financial well-being if something goes wrong. The coverage amount is the maximum sum your insurance company will pay in the event of a claim. When deciding on coverage, it's important to consider the value of the item or situation you're insuring. For example, if you own a bicycle worth $300, you'll want a coverage amount that protects its full value in case of theft or damage.

In this chapter, we've introduced the concept of insurance by drawing parallels to popular social media platforms. By understanding the various types of insurance policies as social media profiles, millennials can begin to see the connections between insurance and their digital lives. In the following chapters, we'll dive deeper into each type of insurance and explore how they relate to specific social media platforms. This will provide a solid foundation for understanding insurance and how it can protect your financial future.

CHAPTER TWO

Life Insurance – The LinkedIn of the Insurance World

Life insurance is comparable to LinkedIn, the professional networking platform where people establish connections, search for job opportunities, and advance their careers. Just as LinkedIn helps you build a strong professional network, life insurance allows you to create a financial safety net for your loved ones in case of your untimely demise. This safety net ensures that your family's financial needs are taken care of, just as a strong professional network helps you secure job opportunities and advance in your career.

LinkedIn is an online platform where professionals from various industries connect, share ideas, and explore job opportunities. As a digital business card, LinkedIn enables you to showcase your skills, experiences, and achievements to potential employers, clients, and partners. By using LinkedIn effectively, you can build a strong professional network that can help you find better job opportunities, create lasting business relationships, and gain valuable insights from industry experts.

A financial safety net refers to having enough money saved or invested to cover unexpected expenses, emergencies, or job losses. It also involves having access to resources that can help you maintain financial stability in times of need. Life insurance is one such resource that can significantly contribute to building a financial safety net for you and your loved ones.

To understand the connection between professional networking on LinkedIn and building a financial safety net through life insurance for teens, let's break down the process into several components.

Building a Strong Profile:

Creating a comprehensive and professional LinkedIn profile that showcases your skills, education, and work experiences is crucial. A well-crafted profile increases your chances of being noticed by potential employers, leading to better job opportunities and higher income. This, in turn, enables you to save and invest more money, including purchasing life insurance policies that can contribute to your financial safety net.

Networking and Connecting with Professionals:

LinkedIn allows you to expand your professional network and gain valuable insights and advice from experienced professionals in your industry. By actively engaging with others, you can make better career decisions, find new job opportunities, and even discover potential business partners or clients. A robust professional network can lead to increased financial stability as you progress in your career, helping you accumulate more savings and investments, including life insurance policies.

Staying Updated on Industry Trends and Opportunities:

By following companies, joining groups, and engaging with relevant content on LinkedIn, you can stay informed about the latest developments in your field. This knowledge helps you make better career choices, identify potential job opportunities, and even inspire you to start your own business. Staying updated on industry trends and opportunities contributes to building a financial safety net through life insurance, as it allows you to seize opportunities that can lead to higher income and financial stability.

Continuous Learning and Skill Development:

LinkedIn offers various resources for learning and skill development, such as LinkedIn Learning. By continuously learning and developing your skills, you can stay relevant in your industry, leading to better job opportunities and increased earning potential. Investing in your education and skill development is a critical aspect of building a financial safety net. As you become more skilled and knowledgeable, you will be better equipped to navigate the job market and secure higher-paying positions that enable you to save and invest more money, including purchasing life insurance policies.

Job Hunting and Career Advancement:

LinkedIn is a powerful tool for job hunting and career advancement. With the platform's job search feature, you can find job openings tailored to your skills and preferences. By actively searching for and applying to relevant positions, you increase your chances of securing a better job with higher pay. This additional income can be used to purchase life insurance policies, strengthening your financial safety net.

Two primary types of life insurance policies are term life and whole life. Understanding the differences between these policies is crucial for making an informed decision about the best option for your needs.

Term life insurance can be thought of as the "job seekers" of the insurance world. These policies offer protection for a specific period, usually between 10 and 30 years, just as job seekers often look for employment opportunities that align with their short-term and long-term career goals. Term life insurance provides a death benefit to your beneficiaries if you pass away during the term, helping them maintain their financial stability. However, if you outlive the term, the policy expires, and you'll need to purchase a new one or convert it to a permanent policy.

Job postings on LinkedIn represent the available opportunities for job seekers within a specific timeframe. Similarly, the term length in a term life insurance policy determines the duration of the coverage. Just as job seekers search for positions that suit their career goals and fit their desired employment duration, individuals seeking term life insurance choose a term length that aligns with their financial goals and protection needs, such as covering a mortgage or ensuring financial stability for their children until they become independent.

LinkedIn's resume building tools help job seekers showcase their skills, experiences, and qualifications to potential employers. A well-crafted resume increases the chances of getting hired, but job seekers must invest time and effort into creating it. Similarly, the premiums in a term life insurance policy represent the cost of obtaining coverage. Policyholders must carefully evaluate and choose a policy with affordable premiums that still provide sufficient protection for their beneficiaries. Just as a resume should highlight the job seeker's strengths, the term life insurance policy's premiums should reflect the policyholder's financial capabilities and coverage needs.

Networking opportunities on LinkedIn allow job seekers to connect with potential employers, colleagues, and industry professionals, increasing their chances of landing a job. In the context of term life insurance, the beneficiaries are the individuals who will receive the death benefit if the policyholder passes away during the term. Networking can be compared to selecting beneficiaries, as both involve building relationships and choosing the right people to support one's goals. Just as job seekers aim to create a strong network to secure a job, term life insurance policyholders designate beneficiaries to ensure their loved ones are financially protected in the event of their passing.

In term insurance, you pay a premium, which is kind of like the fee you pay to keep your insurance coverage active. These premiums are usually lower than other types of life insurance because term insurance only offers protection in case something happens to you, without any additional investment features. For job seekers, think of the premium as the money you'd spend on creating an awesome resume and portfolio that showcases your skills and experiences. Just like paying the insurance premium keeps your coverage going, a well-made resume and portfolio can increase your chances of getting a job.

The policy term in term insurance is how long the insurance covers you. If something happens to you during that time, your family will receive a payout to help them financially. For job seekers, this policy term is like the time you spend looking for a job. Just as term insurance covers you for a set period, you'll spend time and effort searching for a job within a specific timeframe.

In term insurance, the death benefit is the money paid to your family if something happens to you during the policy term. This benefit helps your family financially when you're not around. For job seekers, the death benefit is like getting a job offer with a nice salary. Just like the death benefit supports your family, a well-paying job gives you financial stability and opportunities to grow.

Term insurance doesn't give you any money if you outlive the policy term, which means you don't get any payout when the term ends. For job seekers, this is like continuing to search for better job opportunities even after getting a job. Just as there's no payout at the end of the term in term insurance, you might not always find the perfect job right away and may keep looking for something better.

Whole life insurance is like the "entrepreneurs" of the insurance world, offering lifelong protection and additional financial benefits. Just as entrepreneurs invest in their businesses for long-term growth, whole life insurance is a long-term investment in your family's financial security. These policies not only provide a death benefit but also accumulate a cash value over time, which can be borrowed against or used for other financial needs. Although whole life insurance premiums are typically higher than term life premiums, the lifelong coverage and cash value component make it a valuable financial planning tool.

LinkedIn's company pages enable businesses to establish a brand presence and promote their products or services over the long term. This is similar to the lifelong coverage provided by whole life insurance policies. Just as a company page serves as a platform for businesses to grow and evolve over time, whole life insurance ensures financial protection for the policyholder's beneficiaries regardless of when the policyholder passes away, as long as premiums are paid.

Targeted advertising on LinkedIn allows businesses to reach specific audiences, promoting growth and enhancing visibility. This can be compared to the cash value component in whole life insurance policies. As the cash value accumulates over time, policyholders can use it to enhance their financial standing, borrow against it, or even make withdrawals under certain circumstances. Like targeted advertising that helps businesses reach the right customers and achieve long-term growth, the cash value component of whole life insurance offers flexibility and financial opportunities for policyholders throughout their lives.

Content publishing on LinkedIn involves sharing valuable information, insights, and expertise, which helps businesses establish themselves as industry leaders and build credibility. Similarly, the premium payments in whole life insurance policies not only provide lifelong coverage but also contribute to the policy's cash value. Just as businesses invest time and resources in creating quality content to strengthen their brand image, policyholders must consistently make premium payments to maintain their whole life insurance coverage and grow the cash value. The premiums for whole life insurance are typically higher than term life insurance, reflecting the long-term commitment and financial benefits of the policy.

In some whole life insurance policies, guaranteed additions are bonuses added to the policy every year for a specific period. These additions help increase the policy's overall maturity value. For entrepreneurs on LinkedIn, this can be compared to consistent business growth through expanding their network, acquiring new clients, and exploring new opportunities.

A reversionary bonus in whole life insurance is a periodic bonus declared by the insurance company, based on its performance. This bonus is added to the policy's maturity value and helps increase the overall payout. For LinkedIn entrepreneurs, this is similar to the increased brand visibility they gain through posting relevant content, engaging with their audience, and showcasing their expertise on the platform.

A terminal bonus is an additional bonus paid at the end of a whole life insurance policy's term, which rewards policyholders for maintaining the policy until maturity. This bonus adds to the overall payout received by the policyholder. For entrepreneurs on LinkedIn, this can be likened to achieving long-term business success through consistent networking, building a strong reputation, and delivering exceptional services or products to their clients.

Some whole life insurance policies offer a loyalty bonus, which is an additional payout provided to policyholders who have maintained their policies for a specific period. This bonus recognizes and rewards the policyholder's commitment to the insurance company. For LinkedIn entrepreneurs, this can be compared to the value of retaining clients and building long-term relationships. By providing excellent service and nurturing these relationships, entrepreneurs can enjoy continued business success and client loyalty.

ULIPs, or Unit-linked insurance plans, offer a unique combination of insurance coverage and investment options, similar to how versatile freelancers balance multiple skills and income streams. Just as freelancers adapt to different roles and projects based on their diverse skill sets, ULIPs provide policyholders with the flexibility to customize their insurance and investment strategies according to their financial goals, risk tolerance, and changing needs.

ULIPs provide policyholders with the flexibility to customize their investment portfolio based on their risk appetite, financial goals, and investment horizon. They can switch between funds, invest in a combination of debt and equity, or adjust their investment strategy as their needs change over time. Freelancers on LinkedIn also enjoy flexibility in their professional lives, as they can offer a variety of services, work on multiple projects, and adapt to different roles. LinkedIn provides freelancers with tools to showcase their skills, connect with potential clients, and access job opportunities that suit their expertise.

ULIPs combine life insurance protection with the potential for wealth creation through investment in market-linked assets, such as stocks, bonds, or mutual funds. This dual benefit of insurance and investment is akin to freelancers on LinkedIn, who often have diverse skill sets that enable them to work on different projects and generate multiple income streams. Just as ULIPs offer a comprehensive financial solution, freelancers on LinkedIn leverage their versatile capabilities to cater to a wide range of clients and industries.

ULIPs are designed for long-term commitment, as they typically have a lock-in period of 5 years and encourage policyholders to stay invested for an extended period to maximize returns. Freelancers on LinkedIn also focus on long-term growth and skill development. They continuously update their skills, engage in professional networking, and access learning resources to stay relevant in the ever-evolving job market. Just as ULIPs help policyholders achieve their long-term financial goals, freelancers on LinkedIn invest in their career development to secure future opportunities and growth.

ULIPs offer transparency in terms of charges, investment performance, and policy details, allowing policyholders to monitor their investments and make informed decisions. Similarly, freelancers on LinkedIn can track their work performance through their portfolio and client feedback. This allows them to identify areas for improvement, adapt to changing market demands, and refine their service offerings.

Just as ULIP policyholders can assess their investments' performance and make adjustments as needed, freelancers on LinkedIn use performance data to optimize their professional services and enhance their value to clients.

The premium allocation charge in a ULIP is a percentage of the premium that is deducted upfront before allocating the remaining amount to investment funds. This charge is used to cover administrative expenses and commissions. For freelancers on LinkedIn, this can be compared to the LinkedIn Premium subscription, which is an additional cost that provides access to premium features such as InMail, advanced search filters, and more visibility in job searches.

The fund management charge in a ULIP is a fee levied by the insurance company for managing the investment funds. This charge is usually calculated as a percentage of the fund's net asset value (NAV). Freelancers on LinkedIn also incur costs for using online tools and software to manage their projects, such as project management software, design tools, or productivity apps. These tools help them deliver high-quality work to clients and manage their business effectively.

Policy administration charge in a ULIP is a fee that covers the administrative costs associated with managing the policy, such as paperwork and record-keeping. Freelancers on LinkedIn have their own set of business expenses and overheads, including office supplies, equipment, and utilities. These costs are necessary for running their freelance business and maintaining a professional presence on the platform.

The mortality charge in a ULIP is the cost of providing life insurance coverage to the policyholder. This charge is based on factors such as age, gender, and health status. For freelancers on LinkedIn, this can be compared to the cost of skill development and training, as they continuously invest in their professional growth to stay relevant and competitive in the job market. This may include attending workshops, conferences, or enrolling in online courses.

The surrender charge in a ULIP is a fee levied if the policyholder decides to discontinue the policy before the end of the lock-in period (usually 5 years). This charge is meant to discourage premature withdrawals. Freelancers on LinkedIn may also experience a loss of income if they fail to complete projects on time or if a client cancels a project. This potential loss serves as an incentive for them to manage their time and workload effectively to avoid such situations.

Finding Your Perfect Professional Fit Selecting the right life insurance policy is similar to finding the perfect job opportunity or starting your own business. You need to consider your current financial situation, long-term goals, and the needs of your loved ones. Term life insurance may be the right fit if you're looking for affordable coverage for a specific period, while whole life insurance may be more suitable if you're interested in lifelong protection and additional financial benefits.

CHAPTER THREE

Health Insurance – The Instagram of Protection

In today's digital age, social media platforms like Instagram are an integral part of our daily lives. They help us stay connected, share our experiences, and even inspire us to lead healthier lifestyles. In this chapter, we will explore the concept of health insurance as the Instagram of protection. By drawing parallels between the features of Instagram and the components of health insurance, we aim to provide an easy-to-understand, relatable, and engaging perspective on health insurance for the younger generation.

Filters on Instagram allow users to enhance their photos and express their unique style. Similarly, health insurance policies can be customized according to individual needs, preferences, and budgets. Policyholders can choose the level of coverage, deductibles, copayments, and add-on benefits that suit their specific requirements, ensuring a personalized insurance plan that provides optimal protection.

Stories and Preventive Care:

Instagram Stories are a popular way for people to share what they are doing and keep others updated on their daily activities. Just like how Instagram Stories encourage users to stay active and engaged, health insurance policies often include preventive care benefits to help individuals stay healthy and take care of themselves.

Preventive care benefits usually include regular checkups with a doctor, screenings for illnesses or diseases, and vaccinations to prevent illnesses. By taking advantage of these benefits, individuals can catch health problems early and prevent them from becoming more serious or requiring more expensive treatment later on.

Just like how Instagram Stories can help you stay connected with friends and family, preventive care can help you stay connected to your health and make informed decisions about your well-being. So, don't forget to take advantage of the preventive care benefits offered by your health insurance policy!

Likes, Comments, and Community Support:

On Instagram, likes and comments show that people are interested in and supportive of your content.

Similarly, health insurance provides a network of healthcare providers and resources to support your health needs. This network can include hospitals, clinics, doctors, and specialists that you can turn to for medical care and advice. Having access to a reliable community of healthcare providers can give you peace of mind knowing that you have the support you need when it comes to your health. It's important to choose a health insurance policy that offers a strong network of providers to ensure that you receive quality care when you need it.

Influencers and Wellness Programs:

Instagram influencers often inspire and motivate users to lead healthier lifestyles by sharing tips and insights on nutrition, exercise, and mental well-being. Health insurance providers emphasize wellness by offering programs and incentives that encourage policyholders to adopt healthier habits. From gym membership discounts to rewards for meeting health goals, these wellness initiatives help individuals make lasting changes in their lives, leading to improved health outcomes and reduced healthcare costs.

Hashtags and Awareness Campaigns:

Hashtags on Instagram help users discover new content, trends, and communities, and play a crucial role in raising awareness about various causes and issues. Health insurance providers use awareness campaigns to educate the public about the importance of insurance coverage, the benefits of preventive care, and the need to take control of one's health. Through these campaigns, insurance companies strive to demystify health insurance and empower individuals to make informed choices.

Advertisements and Policy Comparison:

Instagram ads enable businesses to reach their target audience with relevant and engaging content. When searching for the right health insurance policy, individuals must compare different plans and options to find the one that best meets their needs. Online platforms and aggregator websites can help simplify this process, providing side-by-side comparisons of policies, premiums, coverage, and other factors. By taking the time to research and evaluate different plans, individuals can make well-informed decisions and secure the best possible protection for themselves and their families.

Here's an explanation of various health insurance features using analogies with Instagram tools to make it easier to understand:

Room Rent: Instagram Bio

The room rent in a health insurance policy is similar to the Instagram bio. Just as the bio represents a user's key information and identity, room rent is a crucial aspect of health insurance that determines the type of hospital room a policyholder can opt for during their stay. Different policies may have varying room rent limits, which can impact the overall coverage and cost of the plan.

Inclusions: Instagram Posts

Inclusions in a health insurance policy are like Instagram posts. These posts represent the different aspects of a user's life that they choose to share. Similarly, inclusions are the medical expenses and services that the insurance policy covers. Examples of inclusions are hospitalization costs, ambulance charges, daycare procedures, and medication costs. It's essential to understand the inclusions of your health insurance plan to know what is covered and make the best use of your policy.

Exclusions: Archived Instagram Posts

Exclusions in health insurance can be compared to archived Instagram posts. Archived posts are part of a user's account, but they are hidden from public view. Similarly, exclusions are specific medical conditions, treatments, or expenses that the insurance policy does not cover. Examples of exclusions may include cosmetic surgeries, dental treatments, or alternative therapies. Being aware of exclusions helps policyholders avoid unexpected out-of-pocket expenses.

Pre-existing Diseases: Instagram Highlights

Pre-existing diseases in health insurance can be likened to Instagram Highlights. These highlights showcase a user's past events and experiences, which remain easily accessible on their profile. Pre-existing diseases refer to medical conditions that a policyholder has before obtaining health insurance. Insurance companies typically have a waiting period for covering pre-existing diseases, which can vary from one policy to another. It's crucial to consider the waiting period and terms related to pre-existing diseases when choosing a health insurance plan.

Waiting Period: Countdown Sticker on Instagram Stories

The waiting period in a health insurance policy can be compared to the countdown sticker on Instagram Stories. This sticker is used to build anticipation for an upcoming event or milestone. In health insurance, the waiting period is the time that must pass before specific coverage benefits become active. There are different waiting periods for pre-existing diseases, maternity benefits, and certain specified illnesses. Understanding the waiting period helps policyholders manage their expectations and plan for their healthcare needs.

Co-payment: Instagram Shop

Co-payment in health insurance is similar to the Instagram Shop feature. When users make a purchase through the Instagram Shop, they pay a portion of the cost, while the seller covers the rest. Co-payment in health insurance refers to the percentage of medical expenses the policyholder must pay, with the insurance company covering the remaining amount. Co-payment clauses can vary between policies, so it's important to consider them when selecting a health insurance plan.

By using these Instagram tool analogies, we can create a better understanding of health insurance features and make the subject more engaging and relatable, particularly for those who are new to insurance or are just starting to explore their options.

CHAPTER FOUR

Auto Insurance – The Twitter of Transportation

Just like Twitter is an essential part of the social media scene, auto insurance is a crucial aspect of owning a car. Both share the characteristic of being fast-paced and offering diverse content. This chapter will explore the connection between auto insurance and Twitter, making it simpler for teenagers to understand auto insurance.

Retweets and Reimbursements - Understanding Coverage Levels and Options

Auto insurance policies have various coverage levels and options, much like the variety of tweets on Twitter. Retweets spread a message to a broader audience, and different types of coverage provide various levels of financial protection. Here are some common auto insurance coverage options, explained in the context of Twitter:

Liability coverage: This is like a basic tweet that covers you if you cause an accident and hurt someone or damage their property. Most places require this coverage by law.

Collision coverage: Think of this as retweeting with a comment. It protects your car if you get into an accident, no matter who's at fault.

Comprehensive coverage: This is like the pinned tweet on your profile. It covers your car for things not related to accidents, such as theft, vandalism, or natural disasters.

Hashtags and Deductibles - Customizing Your Policy to Fit Your Needs

Hashtags on Twitter help users categorize their tweets and find content that interests them. Similarly, deductibles allow you to customize your auto insurance policy. A deductible is the amount you agree to pay out-of-pocket before your insurance coverage starts. By choosing a higher deductible, you can lower your premium costs (the amount you pay for insurance). It's essential to find a balance between what you can afford and having enough financial protection.

When you're on Twitter, you use hashtags to categorize your tweets and engage with specific topics or trends. This helps make your content more accessible to others interested in the same subjects. Similarly, in the world of auto insurance, deductibles help you tailor your policy to your needs and budget, ensuring that you get the right balance of coverage and cost.

A deductible is the amount you agree to pay out-of-pocket before your insurance coverage kicks in. When you choose a deductible, you're essentially deciding how much financial responsibility you're willing to take on if an accident occurs. By opting for a higher deductible, you can lower your premium costs (the amount you pay for insurance), but you will also have to pay more out-of-pocket in case of a claim. On the other hand, selecting a lower deductible means higher premium costs but less out-of-pocket expenses when filing a claim.

To understand the concept of deductibles better, let's use an example:

Imagine you have an auto insurance policy with a $500 deductible, and you get into an accident that causes $3,000 worth of damage to your car. In this situation, you would pay the first $500 of the repair costs, and your insurance would cover the remaining $2,500.

Now, consider another scenario where you choose a $1,000 deductible instead. If the same accident *occurs, you would pay the first $1,000 of the repair costs, and your insurance would cover the remaining $2,000. However, your premium costs would likely be lower with the higher deductible.*

It's essential to strike a balance when choosing a deductible. You should consider your financial situation, driving habits, and the likelihood of getting into an accident. For example, if you're a cautious driver who rarely gets into accidents, you might opt for a higher deductible to save on premium costs. But if you're a new driver or live in a high-traffic area, you might prefer a lower deductible to minimize your out-of-pocket expenses if an accident occurs.

Ultimately, customizing your policy with the right deductible is like using hashtags effectively on Twitter. Both allow you to personalize your experience, find the right balance, and make the most of the platform or coverage you have.

Tweeting Your Claims - Filing and Managing Auto Insurance Claims

Filing an auto insurance claim might seem scary, but breaking it down into simple steps can make it easier. Here's how to file an auto insurance claim, with a Twitter twist:

Document the accident: Just like capturing a moment in a tweet, it's essential to take photos or videos of the accident scene. Ensure you record the damage to all vehicles involved, the location, and any other relevant details. This documentation will serve as evidence when you file your claim and help your insurance company assess the situation.

Collect information: When interacting with other Twitter users, you exchange messages and follow each other. Similarly, at the scene of an accident, swap contact and insurance information with the other people involved. Collect their names, addresses, phone numbers, and insurance policy numbers. If there are witnesses, get their contact information too.

Report the claim: After gathering all the necessary information, contact your insurance company to inform them about the accident. It's like sending a direct message to resolve an issue on Twitter. Provide your insurer with the details of the incident, the other parties involved, and any supporting documentation like photos or videos. Be honest and accurate when describing the events that led to the accident.

Stay connected: Engaging with your Twitter followers requires regular communication and interaction. Similarly, keep in touch with your insurance company during the claims process. Respond promptly to any requests for additional information or documentation. Maintaining open lines of communication will help ensure a smoother claims process.

Track the claim: On Twitter, you might track the performance of your tweets by checking likes, retweets, and replies. In the same way, monitor the progress of your auto insurance claim. Stay updated on the status of your claim and follow up with your insurance company if you have any questions or concerns.

Complete necessary repairs: Once your insurance company has assessed the damage and approved your claim, it's time to get your vehicle repaired. This is similar to implementing the feedback you receive on Twitter to improve your content. Work with a reputable repair shop and ensure they use quality parts and materials to fix your car.

Trends and Discounts - Maximizing Your Auto Insurance Savings

Like trending topics on Twitter, insurance companies offer various discounts to attract customers. Stay informed about the latest trends in auto insurance discounts and take advantage of these money-saving opportunities. Common discounts include:

Safe driver discount: Having a clean driving record, free of accidents and traffic violations, can qualify you for a safe driver discount. This is similar to having a high-quality Twitter feed, where your tweets are engaging, informative, and well-received by your followers. By practicing safe driving habits, you not only protect yourself and others on the road but also save money on your auto insurance premiums.

Multi-policy discount: Insurance companies often reward customers who bundle multiple policies together, such as auto, home, or renters insurance. This can lead to savings on your overall insurance costs. It's similar to using hashtags on Twitter to streamline your content and make it more discoverable by others. By combining different policies with the same insurance company, you can simplify your insurance management and enjoy lower premiums.

Student and good grades discount: Young drivers who maintain good grades in school may be eligible for discounts on their auto insurance. This reflects a strong and positive Twitter presence, where your tweets demonstrate your dedication, hard work, and ability to balance different aspects of your life. Insurance companies recognize that responsible students are likely to be responsible drivers, so maintaining good academic performance can lead to lower insurance premiums.

Defensive driving course discount: Some insurance companies offer discounts to drivers who complete an approved defensive driving course. This is similar to attending a Twitter workshop or seminar to improve your social media skills. By learning advanced driving techniques and safety strategies, you demonstrate your commitment to being a safer driver, which can lead to savings on your auto insurance.

Low-mileage discount: If you don't drive your car frequently or only cover a limited number of miles, you may qualify for a low-mileage discount. This is akin to being selective with your tweets, focusing on quality over quantity. By driving less, you reduce your risk of being involved in an accident, which can translate to lower insurance premiums.

Anti-theft device discount: Installing anti-theft devices in your car, such as alarms or tracking systems, can also earn you a discount on your auto insurance. This is like using security features on Twitter to protect your account from hackers and other malicious activity. By taking steps to prevent theft or vandalism, you lower the risk for your insurance company, which may lead to lower insurance costs.

CHAPTER FIVE

Home and Renters Insurance – The Facebook of Real Estate

Facebook is a social media platform that connects people worldwide, allowing them to share their lives, experiences, and memories. Similarly, home and renters insurance protect your living space and the valuable possessions within it. By drawing parallels between Facebook and home and renters insurance, this chapter aims to make these insurance types more relatable and easier to understand for teenagers.

Section 1: Timelines and Assets - Protecting Your Property and Possessions

Just as Facebook's timeline feature allows users to document their life events, home and renters insurance policies protect the important milestones related to your living space. By understanding the coverage provided by these insurance types, teenagers can appreciate their importance in safeguarding their property and possessions.

Homeowners insurance:

Dwelling coverage: Dwelling coverage protects the structure of your home, including the walls, roof, and attached structures like a garage or deck. This coverage helps pay for repairs or rebuilding costs if your home is damaged due to a covered peril, such as fire, windstorms, or hail.

Personal property coverage: Personal property coverage protects your belongings inside your home, such as furniture, clothing, and electronics. This coverage helps replace or repair your possessions if they are damaged, destroyed, or stolen due to a covered event. It's essential to create a home inventory to help assess the value of your belongings and ensure you have enough coverage.

Liability coverage: Liability coverage protects you if someone is injured on your property or if you accidentally damage someone else's property. This coverage can help pay for the injured person's medical expenses and your legal defense if you are sued. Additionally, it can cover damage you or your family members cause to someone else's property.

Additional living expenses (ALE) coverage: ALE coverage pays for temporary living expenses if your home becomes uninhabitable due to a covered event, such as a fire or storm. This coverage can help cover the costs of a hotel, meals, and other necessary expenses while your home is being repaired or rebuilt.

Renters insurance:

Personal property coverage: Similar to homeowners insurance, renters insurance covers your belongings inside the rented property. This coverage helps replace or repair your possessions if they are damaged, destroyed, or stolen due to a covered event. As a renter, it's crucial to create an inventory of your belongings to ensure you have adequate coverage.

Liability coverage: Renters insurance also provides liability coverage to protect you if someone is injured in your rental or if you accidentally damage someone else's property. This coverage can help cover medical expenses, legal defense costs, and property damage for which you are responsible.

Additional living expenses coverage: Renters insurance includes additional living expenses coverage, which pays for temporary living expenses if your rental becomes uninhabitable due to a covered event. This can help cover the costs of a hotel, meals, and other necessary expenses while you wait for your rental to be repaired or find a new place to live.

By understanding the different types of coverage provided by home and renters insurance policies, teenagers can gain a better appreciation for the importance of protecting their living spaces and possessions. This knowledge can help them make informed decisions about their insurance needs as they venture into the world of homeownership or renting.

Section 2: Likes, Shares, and Endorsements - Tailoring Your Coverage with Additional Protections

In the same way that Facebook users can like, share, and endorse content to express their preferences and interests, homeowners and renters can customize their insurance policies with additional protections to suit their unique needs. This section will delve into the various add-ons and endorsements that can help teenagers tailor their insurance coverage.

Scheduled personal property endorsement: For valuable items like jewelry, art, or collectibles that exceed the standard limits of personal property *coverage, a scheduled personal property endorsement can provide additional coverage. By appraising and itemizing these high-value possessions, you ensure they are adequately protected in case of damage or theft.*

Replacement cost coverage: Standard insurance policies typically cover the actual cash value of your belongings, which factors in depreciation. Replacement cost coverage, on the other hand, pays for the cost to replace your damaged or stolen items with new ones of similar quality. This add-on can provide more comprehensive protection for your belongings.

Water backup coverage: Standard homeowners and renters insurance policies often exclude damage caused by sewer or drain backups. Adding water backup coverage to your policy can help protect your home and belongings from this type of damage.

Flood insurance: Homeowners and renters insurance policies typically do not cover flood damage. If you live in an area prone to flooding, you may need to purchase a separate flood insurance policy through the National Flood Insurance Program (NFIP) or a private insurer.

Earthquake insurance: Standard insurance policies also exclude earthquake damage. If you live in an earthquake-prone region, you might consider purchasing a separate earthquake insurance policy to protect your home and belongings from potential damage.

Identity theft coverage: With the increasing prevalence of cybercrime, identity theft coverage can be a valuable addition to your insurance policy. This coverage helps cover the costs associated with recovering from identity theft, such as legal fees, lost wages, and credit monitoring services.

Home business coverage: If you run a business from your home, standard homeowners or renters insurance policies may not provide adequate coverage for your business equipment and liability needs. Adding home business coverage to your policy can help protect your business assets and provide liability protection specific to your business operations.

Section 3: Privacy Settings and Insurance Deductibles - Balancing Protection and Affordability

What are deductibles? Think of deductibles like your Facebook privacy settings. A deductible is an amount you agree to pay before your insurance helps out. For example, if you have a $1,000 deductible and something happens that costs $5,000 to fix, you'll pay the first $1,000, and your insurance will cover the remaining $4,000. Deductibles apply to both home and renters insurance policies.

High or low deductibles? Choosing a higher deductible is like setting your Facebook posts to "Friends Only." It can make your insurance more affordable, but you'll have to pay more if something goes wrong. Consider how much money you can spare in case of an emergency when deciding on your deductible.

What's your risk level? Your risk level is how comfortable you are with taking on financial risks. If you don't mind taking some risks, you might be okay with a higher deductible and lower insurance payments. But if you prefer playing it safe, you may want a lower deductible and slightly higher payments to make sure you're well-covered.

Think about your stuff: The value of your home and the things you own plays a role in finding the right deductible, just like the sensitivity of your Facebook posts affects your privacy settings. If you have expensive items or live in a high-value home, you may want a lower deductible for better protection.

Extra coverage: Some insurance policies have separate deductibles for specific situations, like storms, earthquakes, or floods. Keep these extra deductibles in mind when looking for the right balance between protection and cost, just like you would adjust Facebook settings for specific posts or groups.

Check your settings regularly: Just as you should review your Facebook privacy settings from time to time, it's essential to reassess your deductible too. Changes in your finances, the value of your property, or the stuff you own can affect the best deductible level for you.

By understanding insurance deductibles and considering factors like risk level, the value of your belongings, and extra coverages, you can find the perfect balance for your home and renters insurance, just like adjusting your Facebook privacy settings. This balance will give you peace of mind and financial security, making sure you have the coverage you need without breaking the bank.

Section 4: Staying Connected - Managing Your Home and Renters Insurance Policies

Facebook helps people stay connected, and maintaining open communication with your insurance agent is also vital. Regularly reviewing and updating your policies ensures that your coverage remains adequate as your life and possessions change. Here are some tips for managing your home and renters insurance:

Regular check-ins: Think of reviewing your insurance policy as scrolling through your Facebook feed. It's crucial to check your policy at least once a year, just as you would regularly check your Facebook for updates from friends. Annual reviews ensure your coverage remains adequate and up-to-date with your current living situation and possessions.

Home improvements and new purchases: If you make significant home improvements or acquire new high-value items, it's essential to update your insurance policy. Imagine this as updating your Facebook status or adding photos of your latest achievements. Informing your insurance agent about these changes ensures your policy reflects your home's current value and protects your new belongings.

Changes in living situations: Life changes, such as getting a roommate, adopting a pet, or starting a home-based business, can impact your insurance needs. It's like adding a new Facebook friend or joining a new group. Be sure to communicate these changes to your insurance agent, so they can adjust your coverage accordingly.

Discounts and savings: Just as you'd want to take advantage of Facebook's features and tools, you should also explore discounts and savings on your home and renters insurance policies. Talk to your insurance agent about available discounts, like those for installing security systems or bundling multiple policies. This ensures you're getting the best possible deal on your insurance.

Filing claims: When you need to file a claim, it's crucial to stay connected with your insurance company, just as you would keep in touch with friends on Facebook. Promptly report any losses or damages and provide the necessary documentation. Regular communication helps ensure a smoother claims process and a faster resolution.

Building a relationship: Establishing a good relationship with your insurance agent is like building friendships on Facebook. Keep the lines of communication open and ask questions when you're unsure about your coverage. Having a trusted insurance agent to guide you through the complexities of home and renters insurance can give you peace of mind and confidence in your coverage.

By staying connected and actively managing your home and renters insurance policies, teenagers can ensure they have the right protection in place. Regular policy reviews, updating coverage for life changes, and exploring discounts are crucial steps in maintaining adequate insurance coverage. Just as Facebook helps people stay connected and informed, proactive management of insurance policies can lead to better financial security and peace of mind.

CHAPTER SIX

Group Insurance – The YouTube of Collective Protection

Just as YouTube is a platform where people come together to view, share, and engage with a vast array of content, group insurance provides collective protection for a group of individuals under a single policy. In this analogy, we'll explore the connection between group insurance and YouTube, making it simpler for teenagers to understand the concept of group insurance.

Section 1: Channels and Group Policies - Bringing People Together

On YouTube, channels are created by content creators or organizations to share videos with a particular audience. These channels allow people with similar interests to come together, watch, comment, and share their favorite content. Just like YouTube channels, group insurance policies are designed to bring people together under a single umbrella for a common purpose - insurance protection.

Imagine your favorite YouTube channel as your employer or an organization you belong to, like a club or association. They are the ones who initiate and manage the group insurance policy for their employees or members. By being part of the group, you gain access to the insurance benefits, just as you would enjoy watching and engaging with the content on your favorite YouTube channel.

In this context, think of the insurance company as the YouTube platform itself. It provides the necessary infrastructure and support for the group insurance policy to function, just like YouTube enables channels to host and share videos.

So, when you become an employee or a member of an organization with group insurance, you're essentially "subscribing" to a channel that provides insurance benefits instead of videos. By offering group insurance, employers or organizations can provide valuable coverage to multiple people at once, just like a YouTube channel brings together a community of viewers who share common interests.

Section 2: Subscriptions and Premiums - Committing to the Content

Subscribing to a YouTube channel is like showing your support and interest in the content provided by that channel. By subscribing, you'll receive notifications when new videos are uploaded, and you'll have easy access to the channel's content on your homepage. Similarly, when you join a group insurance policy, you commit to participating in the coverage offered by your employer or organization. This commitment involves paying premiums, which are the regular payments made to maintain your insurance coverage.

Think of insurance premiums as the "subscription fee" for your group insurance policy. While YouTube subscriptions are usually free, they still demonstrate your dedication to that particular channel. In the case of group insurance, your premiums represent a financial commitment to maintaining the coverage provided by the policy. Just as the success of a YouTube channel depends on its subscribers and their engagement, the success of a group insurance policy relies on the consistent payment of premiums by its members.

It's worth noting that group insurance premiums are often shared between the employer or organization and the individual members. This arrangement can make insurance more affordable for everyone involved. In a way, this is like sharing the responsibility of supporting a YouTube channel with other subscribers, as everyone contributes to the channel's growth and success.

By comparing group insurance premiums to YouTube subscriptions, we hope to make the concept of insurance payments more accessible and easier for teenagers to understand. Participating in a group insurance policy means making a commitment to protect yourself and your fellow members, much like subscribing to a YouTube channel shows your support for the content and its creator.

Section 3: Playlists and Coverage Options - Customization for Different Needs

Just as YouTube channels use playlists to categorize videos based on themes or interests, group insurance policies provide various coverage options to cater to the unique needs of employees or members. This customization allows individuals to select the protection that best fits their personal circumstances, just as viewers can choose playlists that align with their interests.

To better understand this concept, let's break down the different "playlists" of coverage options that may be available in a group insurance policy:

Health Insurance: Like a playlist featuring all your favorite music, health insurance is the foundation of many group insurance plans. It provides coverage for medical expenses, including doctor visits, hospital stays, and prescription medications. This essential coverage helps ensure that you and your fellow members can access necessary healthcare without the burden of excessive costs.

Dental Insurance: Imagine a playlist that features videos on maintaining a bright, healthy smile. Dental insurance offers coverage for preventive care, such as regular cleanings and checkups, as well as more extensive procedures like fillings, crowns, and orthodontic treatment. By including dental insurance in your group plan, you're helping to promote good oral health for yourself and your fellow members.

Vision Insurance: Vision insurance is like a playlist filled with videos on caring for your eyes and maintaining optimal vision. This coverage option helps pay for eye exams, glasses, and contact lenses, ensuring that you and your fellow members can see clearly and maintain good eye health.

Life Insurance: A playlist featuring inspirational and heartwarming stories could represent life insurance. Life insurance coverage provides financial protection for your loved ones in the event of your passing. By including life insurance in your group plan, you're ensuring that your family has some financial security during a challenging time.

Disability Insurance: Picture a playlist that offers support and resources for overcoming life's obstacles. Disability insurance provides financial assistance if you're unable to work due to illness or injury. This coverage can help you maintain your independence and financial stability during a difficult period.

Section 4: Engagement and Claims - Interacting with the System

In the world of YouTube, viewers engage with content by liking, commenting, sharing videos, and even creating their own content. This interaction is an essential part of the YouTube experience, and it helps to build a sense of community and connection between creators and viewers. Similarly, group insurance policies are designed to benefit employees or members, and engaging with the system is crucial for making the most of your coverage.

To better understand the process of engaging with group insurance, let's compare filing claims to interacting on YouTube:

Watching and Learning: Just as you watch YouTube videos to learn new skills or gain knowledge, it's essential to familiarize yourself with your group insurance policy's coverage and benefits. Read the provided materials, attend informational meetings, or consult with your human resources department to ensure you understand what's covered and how to access your benefits.

Liking and Valuing: When you like a YouTube video, you're showing appreciation for the creator's work. In group insurance, valuing your coverage means taking advantage of the benefits available to you. Schedule regular checkups, use preventive care services, and maintain a healthy lifestyle to get the most out of your insurance plan.

Commenting and Communicating: Commenting on YouTube videos allows you to engage with the creator and share your thoughts or questions. Similarly, communication is vital when it comes to group insurance. If you have questions or concerns about your coverage, don't hesitate to reach out to your insurance provider, human resources representative, or benefits administrator for clarification or assistance.

Sharing and Filing Claims: Sharing a YouTube video helps to spread valuable information or entertainment to others. In group insurance, filing claims is the process of "sharing" your need for coverage with your insurance provider. When you require medical care or other services covered by your policy, submit a claim to access your benefits. It's essential to follow your insurance provider's guidelines for filing claims, including submitting the required documentation within specified timeframes.

By comparing engagement with group insurance policies to interacting on YouTube, we hope to help teenagers better understand the importance of actively participating in their coverage. Just as engaging with YouTube content enhances your viewing experience, taking an active role in understanding and utilizing your group insurance benefits ensures that you receive the protection and support you need.

Section 5: Monetization and Cost Savings - Sharing the Benefits

In this section, we will talk about how group insurance policies can save money for both employers and employees or members, just like how successful YouTube channels can generate revenue for their creators.

When many people join together to buy insurance as a group, it often costs less than if each person bought their own insurance. This is because the insurance company is taking on a larger group of people and spreading the risk among them. The employer or organization often pays a portion of the premium, with the rest of the cost shared by the employees or members.

This shared cost is like how a successful YouTube channel can make money through ads or merchandise. The creator is sharing the benefits of their success with their audience. In the case of group insurance, the cost savings are shared among the members of the group, making it more affordable for everyone.

CHAPTER SEVEN

Travel Insurance – The Snapchat of Adventurous Endeavors

Travel insurance is like the Snapchat of insurance - it's designed to cover you for a specific period, like a trip, and then it's gone. Just like Snapchat, travel insurance offers a temporary solution to a specific need. This chapter will explore the connection between travel insurance and Snapchat and make it easier for teenagers to understand travel insurance.

Section 1: Snapshots and Coverage - Understanding Policy Benefits

Snapchat is a popular social media platform for capturing and sharing memorable moments with friends and family. Similarly, travel insurance is designed to protect you during your travels and give you peace of mind while creating unforgettable memories. Just as Snapchat captures snapshots of your experiences, travel insurance safeguards your trip from unexpected events.

Travel insurance provides coverage for various travel-related risks, including trip cancellation or interruption, medical emergencies, and lost or stolen baggage. It can also offer additional benefits like emergency evacuation, travel assistance, and 24/7 customer support. Having travel insurance can help mitigate the financial impact of these risks and allow you to focus on enjoying your trip.

Section 2: Filters and Fine Print - Decoding Policy Jargon and Exclusions

Snapchat filters are a popular way to make your photos and videos more fun and interesting. However, just like how filters don't change the reality of a situation, travel insurance policies can have exclusions and policy terms that may limit coverage. It's important to understand these terms to ensure that you have the right coverage for your needs.

One common exclusion is pre-existing medical conditions. This means that if you have a medical condition that existed before you purchased your travel insurance policy, such as asthma or diabetes, your policy may not cover any related medical expenses. It's important to disclose any pre-existing conditions to your insurance provider when you purchase your policy to avoid any issues with coverage.

Another common exclusion is adventure sports. If you plan to participate in high-risk activities like bungee jumping or scuba diving, your policy may not cover any injuries sustained during these activities. It's important to review your policy and make sure you have coverage for any activities you plan to participate in.

Policy limits are also important to understand. Each policy has coverage limits, which is the maximum amount that will be paid out in the event of a claim. It's important to review these limits to make sure they are sufficient to cover any potential losses or expenses.

Section 3: Memories and Documentation - Filing and Managing Travel Insurance Claims

When you experience an incident or illness during your travels, it's essential to document everything and contact your insurance provider immediately. This way, you can file and manage your travel insurance claim smoothly. It's like creating a Snapchat story, capturing your travel experiences and sharing them with your friends.

First, call your insurance company as soon as possible and inform them of the incident or illness. They will guide you on the next steps to take, such as collecting receipts and other necessary documentation to support your claim. Take photos of the incident, such as damaged luggage or injuries, to help provide evidence.

After you've submitted your claim, it's important to stay in touch with your insurance company and follow up on any requests for additional information. Think of it like responding to comments on your Snapchat story to engage with your audience. This way, you can ensure that your claim is processed promptly and efficiently.

Section 4: Geofilters and Plan Options - Customizing Your Travel Insurance

Just like Snapchat geofilters add a unique touch to your snaps, travel insurance plan options can be customized to fit your specific travel needs. There are different types of travel insurance plans that you can choose from depending on your situation:

Single trip coverage: This type of plan is designed to cover a single trip or vacation. It's ideal for people who don't travel frequently or have a specific trip planned.

Multi-trip coverage: This plan covers multiple trips within a specific period, usually a year. It's a good option for people who travel often for work or pleasure and want to ensure they have coverage for all their trips.

Group coverage: This type of plan covers a group of travelers, such as a family or a school group. It can provide cost savings and convenience for groups traveling together.

When choosing a travel insurance plan, it's essential to consider your travel needs and the specific risks associated with your trip. For example, if you plan to engage in adventure activities like skiing or hiking, you may want to consider a plan that covers adventure sports. Similarly, if you have pre-existing medical conditions, you should look for a plan that covers them. Customizing your travel insurance plan can ensure that you have the coverage you need for a worry-free trip.

Section 5: Streaks and Loyalty Programs - Maximizing Your Travel Insurance Savings

Snapchat streaks are a fun way to keep track of how long you and your friends have been snapping back and forth. Similarly, travel insurance loyalty programs can reward your loyalty to an insurance provider. These programs offer benefits like discounts, rewards, and perks to customers who stay with the same company. For example, you may be offered a discount for renewing your policy or for being with the company for a certain period. You may also earn rewards points for participating in wellness programs or completing travel surveys. Some programs even offer perks like waived deductibles or additional coverage for loyal customers. By taking advantage of loyalty programs, you can maximize your travel insurance savings and get more out of your coverage.

CHAPTER EIGHT

Digital Tools and Resources for Insurance Management

In today's digital age, managing your insurance policies has never been easier thanks to the availability of various digital tools and resources. These resources can help you stay on top of your coverage and make informed decisions about your insurance needs.

Here are some digital tools and resources for insurance management:

Just like you use social media apps to stay connected with your friends and family, you can use digital tools to keep track of your insurance policies, premiums, and claims.

For example, there are mobile apps and online portals provided by insurance companies that allow you to view your policy details, update your information, and file claims right from your smartphone or computer. Some insurance companies also offer chatbots or virtual assistants that can help answer your questions and guide you through the process of managing your insurance.

In addition, there are third-party websites and apps that can help you compare insurance policies from different companies and find the best coverage and rates for your needs. These tools often use algorithms and data analysis to provide personalized recommendations based on your age, location, and other factors.

Overall, digital tools and resources can make managing your insurance much more convenient and efficient, giving you more time to focus on the things that matter most to you.

Nowadays, there are mobile apps available that can help you manage your insurance policies easily. For example, popular insurance companies like Geico and Allstate have created apps that allow you to view your policy information, make payments, and file claims all from your phone. This means you don't have to sit in front of a computer or make a phone call to take care of your insurance needs.

Using these apps can also be very convenient because you can manage your policies on-the-go, whether you're waiting for a bus, hanging out with friends, or on a road trip. It saves you time and energy by giving you quick access to all the information you need. Plus, these apps often send you reminders and notifications to keep you up-to-date on your policy and payments.

Overall, mobile apps for insurance management can be very useful for teenagers who want to take control of their insurance needs and make sure they are properly covered in case of an emergency.

Online portals are websites created by insurance companies to help policyholders manage their policies. These portals allow you to access your policy information, make payments, and file claims online.

To use an online portal, you need to create an account with your insurance company and provide some basic information about yourself and your policy. Once you've created an account, you can log in anytime to manage your insurance policies.

The benefits of using an online portal for insurance management include the convenience of being able to access your policy information and make changes anytime, anywhere. You can also view your policy documents and coverage details online, which can help you stay organized and informed about your insurance policies.

Using an online portal also allows you to manage multiple policies from different insurance companies in one place, which can save you time and hassle. For example, if you have auto insurance from one company and home insurance from another, you can manage both policies through their respective online portals.

Overall, online portals for insurance management provide a convenient and efficient way to manage your insurance policies and stay informed about your coverage.

Comparison websites are like shopping sites, but instead of clothes or gadgets, they help you compare different insurance policies from different companies. These websites let you enter details about yourself and what type of insurance you are looking for, such as car insurance or health insurance. Then, the website will show you a list of insurance policies from different companies that match your needs.

The list of policies will show you information about what each policy covers, how much it costs, and what customers are saying about it. This makes it easy for you to compare the policies side by side and choose the one that best suits your needs and budget.

Using comparison websites for insurance policy shopping can be really helpful because it saves you time and effort. You don't have to go to each insurance company's website or call them one by one to get information about their policies. Instead, you can find everything in one place and make an informed decision based on your needs and budget.

Online communities for insurance advice and support are virtual spaces where people can come together to share their experiences, ask questions, and get advice related to insurance. These communities can be in the form of forums, social media groups, or online chat rooms.

In these communities, users can seek advice and support related to managing insurance policies, finding the best coverage, and dealing with insurance claims. For example, if someone is having trouble understanding the terms of their policy, they can ask other members of the community for help in interpreting it. If someone is looking for a new insurance policy, they can ask for recommendations or read reviews from other users who have similar needs.

One of the benefits of using online communities for insurance advice and support is the ability to connect with others who have similar insurance needs and challenges. This can be particularly helpful for teenagers who may be new to managing their own insurance policies and may not have a lot of experience with insurance-related issues.

Additionally, online communities are often available 24/7, so users can access them at any time, from anywhere. This makes it easy to get quick answers to questions or find support during times of need.

Overall, online communities for insurance advice and support can be a valuable resource for teenagers who are looking to better understand and manage their insurance policies. By connecting with others who have similar experiences, they can learn more about insurance and find support when they need it most.

CHAPTER NINE

The Future of Insurance – Insurtech, Blockchain, and Beyond

The insurance industry has been around for centuries, and it has evolved significantly over time. Today, we are seeing the emergence of new technologies that are transforming the way insurance is done. This chapter explores the future of insurance and the impact of insurtech, blockchain, and other emerging technologies.

Insurtech refers to the use of technology to improve and streamline the insurance industry. One of the main benefits of insurtech is that it can help insurers to better understand and serve their customers. For example, some companies are using artificial intelligence to analyze customer data and identify patterns that can be used to offer more personalized coverage.

Artificial intelligence (AI) is a technology that allows machines to perform tasks that typically require human intelligence, such as decision making, problem-solving, and learning. In recent years, the insurance industry has started to use AI to improve its processes and provide better services to customers.

One way AI is used in insurance is to automate claims processing. When a customer files a claim, AI-powered software can quickly review the information, such as the nature of the claim and any supporting documents, to determine if it is valid. This process is faster and more accurate than manual review, which can take longer and be prone to errors.

AI is also used to improve risk assessment, which is the process of determining the likelihood of a particular event happening, such as a car accident or home break-in. By analyzing large amounts of data, including past claims and demographic information, AI algorithms can identify patterns and make more accurate predictions about future risks. This allows insurance companies to offer more customized policies and pricing, based on a customer's specific risk profile.

Another area where AI is being used in insurance is in chatbots and virtual assistants. These tools use natural language processing, a type of AI that allows computers to understand and respond to human language, to assist customers with their insurance needs. For example, a customer can use a chatbot to ask questions about their policy or file a claim, without needing to speak to a human agent.

Overall, the use of AI in insurance has the potential to improve efficiency, accuracy, and customer experience. However, it is important to ensure that AI is used ethically and transparently, to avoid unintended consequences and maintain customer trust.

Another area where insurtech is having an impact is in claims management. Insurtech companies are developing new tools and platforms that make it easier for customers to file claims and for insurers to process them. This includes things like mobile apps that allow customers to file claims from their smartphones and software that can automatically assess damage to property.

Blockchain is another technology that is poised to transform the insurance industry. Blockchain is a distributed ledger that allows for secure and transparent transactions. In insurance, blockchain can be used to create smart contracts that automatically execute when certain conditions are met. This could eliminate the need for intermediaries and reduce the risk of fraud.

Blockchain technology is essentially a digital ledger that allows for secure and transparent transactions to take place without the need for a centralized *authority. This means that transactions can be recorded and verified in a secure and efficient manner, without the need for intermediaries such as banks or government institutions.*

In the context of insurance, blockchain technology has the potential to revolutionize the industry by providing greater transparency and security for policyholders, insurers, and other stakeholders. Here are some examples of how blockchain technology is being used in insurance:

Claims management: Blockchain technology can be used to streamline the claims process by providing a secure and transparent platform for policyholders to file claims and insurers to process them. This can help reduce fraud and errors in the claims process, while also providing greater transparency for policyholders.

Underwriting: Blockchain technology can be used to provide greater transparency and accuracy in the underwriting process. By using data from a variety of sources, including social media and IoT devices, insurers can better assess risk and provide more personalized policies.

Smart contracts: Smart contracts are self-executing contracts with the terms of the agreement between buyer and seller being directly written into lines of code. Blockchain technology enables smart contracts to be executed in a secure and transparent manner, which can be used to automate the insurance process and reduce the need for intermediaries.

Fraud prevention: Blockchain technology can be used to prevent fraud by providing a secure and transparent platform for recording and verifying transactions. This can help insurers detect and prevent fraudulent claims, which can save them money and reduce premiums for policyholders.

One area where blockchain is already being used is in the sharing economy. Companies like Airbnb and Uber are partnering with insurers to provide coverage to their users. With blockchain, the insurance policies can be automatically activated and deactivated based on the user's activity.

Smart contracts are a new and innovative way of managing agreements between parties. In the insurance industry, smart contracts have the potential to revolutionize the claims process, making it faster, more efficient, and more transparent. In this article, we will discuss the use of smart contracts in insurance and how they can benefit both insurers and policyholders.

Smart contracts are self-executing agreements that use blockchain technology to automate the process of verifying and enforcing the terms of a contract.

They operate on a set of predetermined rules and conditions that are stored on a blockchain network, allowing for automatic execution of the contract when certain conditions are met.

In the insurance industry, smart contracts can be used to automate the claims process. When a policyholder submits a claim, the smart contract automatically verifies the claim and initiates the payment process if the claim is approved. This eliminates the need for manual processing and reduces the risk of fraud, as the contract is programmed to only pay out under certain conditions.

Smart contracts can also be used to automate policy issuance and renewal. Instead of relying on traditional paperwork and manual processing, smart contracts can automatically generate and issue policies based on pre-defined rules and conditions.

One of the main benefits of smart contracts in insurance is increased efficiency. The automation of the claims process and policy issuance reduces the need for manual processing and eliminates the potential for human error, resulting in a faster and more streamlined process.

Smart contracts also increase transparency and reduce the risk of fraud. The predetermined rules and conditions of the contract are stored on a blockchain network, making it impossible to alter or manipulate the terms of the contract. This increases trust between insurers and policyholders, as both parties have access to the same information.

In addition to insurtech and blockchain, other emerging technologies are also poised to have an impact on the insurance industry. For example, the Internet of Things (IoT) is allowing insurers to collect more data about customers and their behavior. This data can be used to offer more personalized coverage and to price policies more accurately.

The Internet of Things (IoT) is changing the way we live and work, and it is also transforming the insurance industry. By collecting data from connected devices, such as sensors and wearables, insurance companies are able to offer more personalized policies and better manage risk. Here's how IoT is being used in the insurance industry:

Risk management: Insurance companies are using IoT devices to monitor risk and prevent losses. For example, sensors can be placed in homes or vehicles to detect potential hazards and alert homeowners or drivers before an accident occurs. This can help prevent accidents and reduce insurance claims.

Health monitoring: Wearables, such as fitness trackers and smartwatches, can collect health data that insurers can use to offer more personalized policies. For example, insurers can use data from wearables to monitor a person's fitness level and adjust their life insurance premiums accordingly.

Telematics: Insurers are using telematics devices to collect data on driving behavior, such as speed, acceleration, and braking. This data is then used to offer usage-based insurance policies, which adjust premiums based on how often and how well a person drives.

Property insurance: IoT devices can be used to monitor homes and buildings for potential damage, such as leaks or fires. Insurance companies can use this data to offer more comprehensive and accurate property insurance policies.

Claims processing: IoT devices can also be used to speed up the claims process. For example, if a car is in an accident, the telematics device can provide information about the accident, such as the speed at impact, which can help insurers determine fault and process claims more quickly.

Overall, the use of IoT in insurance is improving risk management, reducing costs, and providing more personalized policies for customers. As the technology continues to develop, we can expect to see even more innovative uses of IoT in the insurance industry.

CHAPTER TEN

Evolution of Insurance Industry

Insurance has been a vital part of modern society for centuries. It provides individuals and businesses with financial protection against unforeseen risks and losses. The insurance industry has evolved significantly over the years, from its beginnings in ancient civilizations to its current state as a global industry worth trillions of dollars. In this book, we will explore the evolution of the insurance industry, its history, and its current state worldwide.

Early History of Insurance

Insurance as a concept has been around for a long time, dating back to ancient times. One of the earliest known examples of insurance can be traced back to the Babylonian civilization, where traders would take out loans to finance their shipments. If their shipments were lost or stolen, they would not have to pay back the loan. This was essentially a form of insurance that protected the traders from financial losses.

The Chinese also had a similar system of insurance, known as the "yao hui," which was a form of mutual aid society. Members of the society would contribute money to a common fund, which would be used to compensate any member who suffered a loss.

In ancient Greece and Rome, burial societies were common. These societies would pay for the funeral expenses of their members, ensuring that their loved ones would not have to bear the financial burden of their passing.

The concept of insurance continued to evolve over time. In the 14th century, marine insurance became popular in Europe, where merchants would take out policies to protect against losses from shipwrecks, pirates, and other perils of the sea.

In the 17th century, the first insurance company was established in England, called the Hand in Hand Fire and Life Insurance Society. This marked the beginning of the modern insurance industry, which has continued to evolve and grow over the centuries.

Today, insurance is an integral part of our lives, protecting us from financial losses due to accidents, illness, and other unforeseen circumstances. The history of insurance shows how it has evolved over time to meet the changing needs of society, and it will continue to adapt and change in the future.

The Emergence of Modern Insurance

The modern insurance industry as we know it today started in the late 17th century in London, England with the creation of Lloyd's of London. This was a group of merchants who would come together and pool their money to insure cargo ships traveling across the ocean. This helped to reduce the risk of loss from shipwrecks or other disasters.

As the years went by, other forms of insurance emerged, including life insurance and fire insurance. Life insurance policies would pay out money to the family of the policyholder if they were to die unexpectedly. Fire insurance policies would protect against losses due to fires, which were a common occurrence at the time due to the use of open flames for lighting and cooking.

In the 19th century, liability insurance became popular. This type of insurance protected businesses and individuals from being sued for damages or injuries caused to others. For example, if someone slipped and fell on a wet floor in a store, the liability insurance policy would cover the costs of the person's medical bills and any other damages awarded in a lawsuit.

The growth of the modern insurance industry was also influenced by the Industrial Revolution, which led to the development of new technologies and industries. Insurance companies began to offer policies specifically designed for the needs of businesses and factories, such as worker's compensation insurance and property insurance for factories and warehouses.

Overall, the emergence of modern insurance helped to protect individuals and businesses against unexpected losses and provided a sense of security and stability.

The Development of Insurance Regulation

As the insurance industry expanded, there was a growing concern about the need for regulation to protect policyholders from fraudulent or unscrupulous insurance companies. In the United States, the first state insurance department was established in New Hampshire in 1851. However, it wasn't until the early 20th century that insurance regulation became more widespread.

In the United States, the National Association of Insurance Commissioners (NAIC) was established in 1871 as a voluntary association of state insurance commissioners. The NAIC worked to develop uniform insurance regulations and standards across the country. In 1945, the McCarran-Ferguson Act granted states the authority to regulate the insurance industry within their borders.

Similarly, in the United Kingdom, the Insurance Companies Act of 1974 established the framework for insurance regulation. The act created the role of the Chief Insurance Commissioner, who was responsible for overseeing the industry and enforcing regulations.

Today, most countries have some form of insurance regulation in place. These regulatory bodies oversee insurance companies to ensure that they are financially stable and able to pay out claims to policyholders. They also set standards for policy contracts and require insurance companies to disclose information about their policies and financial performance.

The development of insurance regulation has had a significant impact on the industry, as it has helped to increase consumer confidence in insurance products and protect policyholders from fraud and insolvency. However, the regulatory landscape continues to evolve, with new challenges such as emerging technologies and changing consumer expectations requiring ongoing adaptation and reform.

Technology and the Insurance Industry

Technology has played a vital role in shaping the insurance industry in recent years. Insurance companies use various technologies to streamline their operations, improve efficiency and offer better services to customers. One of the earliest technologies used in the insurance industry was computers, which helped to process claims and store policyholder information. With the advent of the internet, online marketplaces for insurance policies started to emerge. This allowed consumers to compare policies from different insurance providers and make informed decisions.

In recent years, the insurance industry has witnessed a significant shift in the adoption of new technologies. Artificial intelligence (AI) is being used to enhance risk assessment, automate underwriting, and improve customer service. AI-powered chatbots are being used to handle customer queries and provide instant support. The internet of things (IoT) is also being used to collect data from sensors in homes and cars to provide better risk assessments and personalized insurance coverage. For instance, car insurance companies use IoT devices to monitor driving habits and offer discounted rates for safe drivers.

Blockchain technology is another emerging technology that is being used to revolutionize the insurance industry. Blockchain is a decentralized, secure ledger that records transactions in a tamper-proof manner.

This technology can be used to automate claims processing, prevent fraud, and reduce costs associated with insurance claims. Insurance companies are exploring the use of blockchain to offer smart contracts, which are self-executing contracts that automatically pay out claims when certain pre-defined conditions are met.

CHAPTER ELEVEN

Insurance in India

Insurance has been an essential part of our lives for centuries, providing financial security and protection against unforeseen circumstances. In India, the insurance industry has undergone significant changes since its inception, and it continues to evolve with the changing needs of the country. This book will explore the history of insurance in India, how it has developed over time, and the current state of the industry.

Early History of Insurance in India

The concept of insurance can be traced back to ancient civilizations in India where merchants and traders would pool their resources to protect against losses from disasters. In fact, the famous Indian epic Mahabharata has a reference to insurance. It is said that Yudhishthira, the eldest Pandava brother, had insured his army with an amount equivalent to the value of his kingdom, against losses that may occur in the war.

During the medieval period, insurance was practiced in the form of Takaful, which was essentially a mutual aid system used to support each other in times of need. Merchants would pool their resources and help each other in case of a loss due to shipwrecks or other disasters.

In the early 1800s, the British East India Company established the first insurance company in India, the Oriental Life Insurance Company in Kolkata, in 1818. The company primarily provided insurance for European settlers in India.

In 1850, the Bombay Mutual Assurance Society was established, which was the first Indian-owned insurance company in the country. The company provided fire insurance for properties and buildings.

In 1912, the Indian Life Assurance Companies Act was passed, which regulated the insurance industry in India and allowed for the establishment of more insurance companies. The Life Insurance Corporation of India (LIC) was established in 1956, which nationalized the life insurance industry in the country. The general insurance industry was nationalized in 1972, and the General Insurance Corporation of India was established to oversee the industry.

The Emergence of Modern Insurance in India

The emergence of modern insurance in India can be traced back to the early 1900s when several Indian-owned insurance companies were established. The first Indian-owned insurance company was the Bombay Mutual Life Assurance Society, which was founded in 1870. This company provided life insurance to Indians who were previously unable to obtain coverage from British-owned insurance companies.

In 1912, the Indian Life Assurance Companies Act was passed by the British government, which regulated the insurance industry in India and allowed for the establishment of more insurance companies. This led to the establishment of several Indian-owned insurance companies, including the Oriental Insurance Company, the New India Assurance Company, and the United India Insurance Company.

During this period, the insurance industry in India was primarily focused on providing life insurance to individuals. The industry was still in its nascent stage and faced several challenges, including low awareness among the general population and limited access to insurance in rural areas.

Despite these challenges, the Indian insurance industry continued to grow and evolve. In the years following independence in 1947, the government of India began to take a more active role in the industry. The Life Insurance Corporation of India (LIC) was established in 1956 through an act of parliament, which nationalized the life insurance industry in the country. The general insurance industry was nationalized in 1972, and the General Insurance Corporation of India was established to oversee the industry.

The nationalization of the insurance industry was aimed at providing affordable insurance to all citizens, especially those in rural areas. It helped increase insurance penetration in the country and provided a stable environment for the industry to grow.

Overall, the emergence of modern insurance in India was a significant development in the country's history. It provided Indians with access to insurance, which was previously limited to British-owned companies. The industry continues to grow and evolve, with the liberalization of the industry in the 1990s and the emergence of digital technology and insurtech startups in recent years.

Nationalization of Insurance in India

After India gained independence in 1947, the government sought to strengthen the country's economic infrastructure, including the insurance industry. Before nationalization, insurance was dominated by foreign companies that catered to the needs of the urban elite. The majority of the Indian population, especially those in rural areas, did not have access to insurance products and services.

To address this issue, the government decided to nationalize the insurance industry. In 1956, the Life Insurance Corporation (LIC) Act was passed, which nationalized the life insurance industry. The act gave the government the power to create a corporation to carry out the business of life insurance in India. The LIC was established as a result, with a mandate to provide affordable insurance to all citizens, especially those in rural areas.

In 1972, the government passed the General Insurance Business (Nationalization) Act, which nationalized the general insurance industry in India. The act established the General Insurance Corporation of India (GIC) to oversee the industry. Four subsidiaries were also created under the GIC, including the National Insurance Company Limited, the New India Assurance Company Limited, the Oriental Insurance Company Limited, and the United India Insurance Company Limited.

The nationalization of the insurance industry was a significant step towards making insurance accessible to all citizens, regardless of their socioeconomic background. It also helped in creating employment opportunities in the industry and generating revenue for the government. However, the nationalization also created a monopoly, leading to inefficiencies and a lack of innovation in the industry.

The government's decision to liberalize the insurance industry in the 1990s was aimed at increasing competition and improving the quality of insurance products and services. Nevertheless, the nationalization of the industry played a crucial role in making insurance accessible to the masses in India.

Liberalization of Insurance in India

In 1991, the Indian government began to liberalize the country's economy and opened up various sectors, including the insurance industry, to private players. This was a significant shift from the earlier policy of having only state-owned insurance companies in the market.

The move to liberalize the insurance industry was driven by the need to improve insurance penetration in the country, which was very low at the time. The monopoly of state-owned companies had resulted in limited product offerings and poor customer service. The opening up of the market to private players was expected to bring in new investments, modern technology, and innovative products.

In 1993, the government allowed private players to enter the industry by issuing licenses to 12 companies. This was followed by the establishment of the Insurance Regulatory and Development Authority (IRDA) in 1999, which was tasked with regulating and promoting the development of the insurance industry in India.

The entry of private players brought in a new wave of competition, leading to better products and services for consumers. Companies started to innovate and offer specialized insurance products such as health insurance, travel insurance, and cyber insurance. They also focused on providing better customer service, using modern technology to improve the customer experience.

The liberalization of the insurance industry in India has led to increased insurance penetration in the country. According to the IRDA, the insurance penetration in India was 3.76% in 2020, up from 2.71% in 2001. The industry has also witnessed a significant increase in the number of policies sold, with the total number of policies increasing from 97 million in 2001 to 328 million in 2020.

Overall, the liberalization of the insurance industry in India has been a positive development, providing consumers with more choices, better products, and improved services. The entry of private players has led to healthy competition, driving innovation and growth in the industry.

Current State of Insurance in India

The insurance industry in India has come a long way since its inception. Today, there are more than 70 insurance companies operating in India, offering a wide range of products and services. The industry has seen significant growth in recent years, with the Insurance Regulatory and Development Authority of India (IRDAI) reporting that the industry's total premium income grew by 11.3% in 2020-21.

One of the biggest changes in the industry has been the growth of private insurance companies. Until the early 2000s, the insurance sector in India was dominated by state-owned companies. However, the

Indian government opened up the industry to private players in 2000, leading to the entry of several private insurance companies. Today, private insurers account for a significant share of the market, with companies like ICICI Prudential, HDFC Life, and SBI Life among the largest players.

Digital technology has also had a significant impact on the insurance industry in India. With the widespread adoption of smartphones and the internet, insurance companies have embraced digital channels to reach customers and provide them with convenient access to insurance products and services. Many insurance companies have developed mobile apps and online portals that allow customers to purchase policies, pay premiums, and file claims online. These digital channels have not only made insurance more accessible to customers but have also helped insurance companies to reduce costs and improve efficiency.

The emergence of insurtech startups has also had a significant impact on the insurance industry in India. These startups are leveraging technology to disrupt traditional insurance models, offering innovative products and services that cater to the changing needs of customers. For example, some insurtech startups are using artificial intelligence and machine learning to develop personalized insurance products that are tailored to the specific needs of individual customers.

The government of India has also taken several steps to increase insurance penetration in the country, especially among underprivileged sections of society. The government's flagship insurance program, Pradhan Mantri Jeevan Jyoti Bima Yojana (PMJJBY), provides life insurance coverage to people below the poverty line. Similarly, the Pradhan Mantri Fasal Bima Yojana (PMFBY) provides crop insurance to farmers at affordable premiums.

Despite the growth and progress in the industry, there are still several challenges that need to be addressed. One of the biggest challenges is the low penetration of insurance in the country, with many people still uninsured or underinsured. The insurance industry in India also needs to do more to educate customers about the importance of insurance and the benefits it provides.

The insurance industry in India has come a long way since its inception in the early 1800s. From the establishment of the first insurance company by the British East India Company to the nationalization of the industry in the mid-20ᵗʰ century and the liberalization of the industry in the 1990s, the industry has undergone significant changes. Today, the industry is growing rapidly, driven by digital technology and the emergence of new players. With the government of India's focus on increasing insurance penetration in the country, the industry is set to become an even more important part of our lives in the years to come.

9 7 9 8 8 9 0 0 2 8 1 1 2